T5-ADX-530

FIRST IN AMERICA

FIRST IN AMERICA
An Education Governor Challenges North Carolina

by Governor James B. Hunt Jr.

First in America Foundation
Raleigh, NC • January 2001

This book was made possible by the generous support of the following companies:

Bank of America

The Belk Foundation

BellSouth

Bernhardt Furniture Company

Blue Cross & Blue Shield of North Carolina

BB&T Corporation

Cone Mills Corporation

First Union Corporation

Food Lion, LLC

Glaxo Wellcome

IBM Corporation

Jefferson Pilot Corporation

Lowe's Companies, Inc.

Lundy Packing Company

Maersk Sealand

Nortel Networks

RJ Reynolds Tobacco Company

Wachovia Corporation

This book is dedicated to my mother, Elsie Brame Hunt, a wonderful English teacher, and to all the teachers and educators of North Carolina

Contents

	Foreword, by Richard W. Riley	ix
	Introduction	1
1.	A Teacher's Son	3
2.	A Truly Audacious Goal	10
3.	*Goal 1.* A Smart Start	17
4.	*Goal 2.* Excellent Teaching	24
5.	Goal 3. Safe Schools	38
6.	*Goal 4.* High Student Performance	47
7.	*Goal 5.* Community Support	58
8.	The Rewards of Mentoring	71
9.	Our Most Important Enterprise	79
10.	What I've Learned	85
	Acknowledgments	89
	About the Author	91

Foreword

"If you don't know where you are going, you surely will never get there." This is true of most things in life, but especially education and our schools. *First in America* is so important that I urge all North Carolinians and other Americans to read it and do their part to turn it into reality in their homes, their schools, and their communities.

I am proud of my good friend Governor Jim Hunt for what he has done and is doing for North Carolina and for America. He understands the critical role better schools play in our future, how to move education forward, and how to build partnerships to make a positive difference.

First in America is an excellent blueprint for better education in North Carolina. Other states, too, could be guided by these recommendations. This action plan contains clear and significant goals for the next ten years. These goals build on the strong, measurable progress that North Carolina has made during the last ten years.

The time to make bold progress is now, at a time when a record number of children are filling North Carolina schools. North Carolina can use the achievements of the last ten years as a springboard to become first in the nation.

The keys to better education are six positive practices that together create and sustain the momentum for change: leadership from the statehouse to the schoolhouse; higher expectations of all our children, including those from disadvantaged families; a comprehensive set of strategies; involvement of families, businesses, and the community; collaboration among all sectors of education from teachers to school boards to universities, and from early childhood to college age; and sustained effort week after week.

This book lays out the challenges and solutions. It calls on all North Carolinians to be part of the solutions. Yes, the challenges are great, the problems are big, and the goals are high. However, the opportunities are enormous, not only for North Carolina's children, but also for all its citizens if everyone pulls together to make the state's schools first in America by 2010.

It is quite simple: Better education is everybody's business, not just today but every day for the next ten years. And North Carolinians know that. My best wishes now and in the years ahead for much success in education in your great state.

Dick Riley

RICHARD W. RILEY
Secretary, U.S. Department of Education

Introduction

AS NORTH CAROLINA enters a new century, we can take pride in the progress we have made in public education. We have come from being among the lowest states in the performance of our students to being above the national average. Now we are poised to go to the top.

But education and our public schools are symbolic of something much bigger. They involve our commitment to each other as a people and our aspirations for the future of our society.

I want North Carolina to have high aspirations. I want us to be audacious. I want us to be first in America in education. If we do this, we will be first in America as a place to live, to raise our children, and to pursue our dreams.

I believe the public schools belong to the people of North Carolina and I've written this book for them. It tells what I've learned. And it sets out how we can be first in America. But doing it will be the biggest test that our state has ever faced.

More than anything else, I want the people of North

Carolina to understand how important this challenge is, what it will take to meet it, and that we *can* meet it.

As people read this book, I hope they will understand the five goals—the five parts of the plan that can make us first. More than that, I hope they will get ideas about what they can do personally to meet this challenge—and be motivated to do it.

Pursuing this effort—this dream—will put us in North Carolina today squarely in the tradition of great efforts in our history. The first European colony was established on our shores in 1584. The first public university in America was created in Chapel Hill in 1793. The first powered flight was made by the Wright brothers at Kitty Hawk in 1903. Now we can be first in America in education by 2010.

Our efforts to meet this challenge can give us a sense of purpose and use our full energies in the decade ahead. And in the process we can truly become a state "where the weak grow strong and the strong grow great."

CHAPTER I

A Teacher's Son

MY MOTHER WAS A TEACHER, a marvelous teacher. She taught English. She loved literature, and she loved to teach. So early in my life I saw what successful teaching was and how all students learned from it, because I saw my mother do it. I saw excellence close up.

Many of the kids she taught were poor. A lot of them didn't have shoes to wear. Plenty of them couldn't afford lunch money, and we didn't have free lunches. They brought a biscuit and maybe a little piece of ham in a paper sack. Some people looked down on poor folks, but my mother never did. She didn't see a student as a poor, dirty child in ragged clothes. She saw what was in her students. She saw their potential to learn. She felt that they all could learn, and she went the extra mile to make sure they did.

That's why I've always had this vision of how teachers can teach well, how students can learn, and how we can have successful schools where all the students are watched out for, taken care of, and expected to do well. It's a vision that has guided me throughout my public life.

It's the reason I went into politics. I wanted to help people have better opportunities. When I was growing up, there weren't many jobs in Wilson County. Most people were in agriculture, and they were paid poorly. Many of the students in my class were children of dirt-poor tenant farmers. I remember being puzzled in January when a lot of my classmates didn't come back to school after Christmas. It turned out their fathers had moved them to another farm in another school district in the hope they could make a little more money, or at least come out even at the end of the year.

When manufacturing jobs started coming to my county, they were low-paying. A lot of the companies had fled from the North to find cheap labor. Many of the leaders in the community then didn't want high-paying jobs to come in, because they didn't want competition for the labor. I didn't think that was right.

I believe in helping all people have a good life, a good job, enough money for their family, and a good future. I learned early on that the only way to have those things for our people is through education—through the public schools.

Every time I ran for Governor, I didn't run just to *be* Governor. I ran to *do* something. In particular, I ran to get something done in education. When I ran for Lieutenant Governor in 1972, I pledged to put in public kindergartens, and we did. I ran for Governor the first time in 1976 saying that every child had to learn to read in the early grades. Many children were being promoted not knowing how to read. So we started the Primary Reading Program, which put teachers' assistants in every classroom in the first, second, and third grades. In 1980 we focused on economic growth and how to be world-competitive.

When I ran again in 1992, I pledged to put in standards and accountability. I was determined that we wouldn't graduate any more students who didn't have the skills to get a good job. And I ran to help every child to get a good start in life.

In 1996 I ran on the platform of raising standards for teachers and raising teachers' pay to the national average. There wasn't anything fuzzy about this platform. People knew exactly what I planned to do. My campaign put my goals in television commercials. I considered those goals to be solemn commitments to the people of North Carolina, and we have kept them. Now, as we enter a new century, North Carolina is on target to achieve all those goals.

A lot of people don't know how much progress we've made in the public schools—or don't believe we've made much, if any. Some people don't want to believe we've made progress because they're down on the public schools.

The fact is, North Carolina's schools are a lot better than many people think they are, and we're making more progress than any other state in the country, especially when you consider where we started.

It's not just me saying that. It's also the National Education Goals Panel, a bipartisan group formed in 1990 by President Bush and the nation's governors, which reported in December 1998 that no state's schools were making more progress in more areas than North Carolina's. That same year *Education Week,* the nation's premier education newspaper, said North Carolina was one of the top twelve states *overall* in education and cited us as one of two states doing the most to put in place real and meaningful accountability measures.

Don't be misled by people who just want to talk about North Carolina's SAT scores. Even the Educational Testing Service, which administers the SAT, says it's not a good measure of the quality of a state's education system. How well students do on the SAT is closely related to how well-educated and well-to-do their families are. Our legacy of poverty, segregation, and poor schools obviously hurts us. Scores on the SAT are also related to the percentage of high school students who take it. About 60 percent of our high school graduates took it in 1999. In my wife's home state of Iowa, only 5 percent took it. If we adjusted for the percentage who take it, North Carolina would go up from forty-eighth in the country to thirty-eighth. As it is, students in our state have made more gains on the SAT in the 1990s than those in any of the thirty-eight states that primarily rely on the SAT for college entrance. Our students' average was up more than 40 points.

The best state-by-state comparison is the National Assessment of Education Progress (NAEP), which began in 1969. It's a national report card, administered by the National Center for Education Statistics within the U.S. Department of Education. It's the only ongoing national assessment of what students know and can do in various subject areas. It showed that in the 1990s our students made the greatest gains among all the states on math tests given to fourth- and eighth-graders. We also did well in reading. For the first time, our students scored right at the national average!

So, as the 1990s were ending, we were making our schools better—a lot better. But as I began my last two years as Governor, I sensed we needed something more. I asked myself: Where do we go from here? How do we keep this progress going? How do we ensure that every child benefits?

I wanted to get people in North Carolina committed to a specific goal. We don't have enough clear goals in our society, and the goals we have aren't high enough. I asked myself: What should the goal be? It should be a goal worthy of our people, worthy of our state, our history, our potential. It should be a high goal that would make us stretch. We shouldn't be satisfied with low goals in North Carolina. We shouldn't try to be just average. Well, then, what do we want? Do we want to just be better than we are now? Should we try to be *among* the best? Or one of the best? No! Our goal should be to be *the best*—to make our schools first in America.

So I decided to issue that challenge to North Carolinians in my final State of the State Address to the legislature on February 1, 1999.

I started the speech by talking about our progress: "North Carolina's not just leading the South, North Carolina's leading the nation in education reform." Then I said:

> If we can make this kind of improvement in this decade, what can we do in the decade ahead?
>
> So as we celebrate our progress, let's resolve to finish what we started. Let's finish building this foundation. Let's not be satisfied with what we've done in this decade.
>
> Let's aim even higher in the next decade.
>
> Let's aim even higher than we have ever dreamed of.
>
> I believe that if we can lead the nation in education progress, we can lead the nation in education—period.
>
> So tonight I am announcing a new initiative to set new goals for our schools. I challenge North Carolinians to raise our sights and raise our schools to an even higher level. Let's commit ourselves to this ambitious goal:
>
> *By the year 2010, North Carolina will build the best system of*

public schools of any state in America. By the end of the first decade of the 21st century, we will be first in education.

You heard me right. The best system of public education in America. The best schools. First in education.

What does that mean? It means being first in preparing our young people for the 21st-century economy. It means being first in educating and equipping them to compete with anybody anywhere. It means being first in outworking and outthinking our competitors across the nation and around the world.

How do we get there by 2010? The same way we got here. First, set clear goals. Then set benchmarks so we can measure our progress and compare ourselves to other states. Then get to work.

To be first in America is a big goal, but it's more than that. It's a challenge—not just to educators, but to all North Carolinians. The educators can't do it alone; it will take all of us working together. So in this book I explain how we get to be first. I share what I've learned about education in my lifetime and my career. And I challenge you—and every North Carolinian—to make a commitment to make our schools the best they can be: for our state, for our children, and for our future.

CHAPTER 2

A Truly Audacious Goal

I REMEMBER WHEN I WAS A STUDENT at North Carolina State University hearing Governor Terry Sanford talk about the "audacious goal" of providing a quality education for every child in North Carolina. That term—"audacious goal"—has stuck with me ever since.

After I was first elected Governor, in 1976, I was working on my first State of the State Address. I went to the library in the Executive Mansion, pulled down all the books about the governors who'd served since 1950, and read what they'd said about education. I was shocked to find that when Terry Sanford was elected Governor in 1960, just sixteen years earlier, North Carolina's dropout rate was 47 percent. That's nearly *half* our students dropping out!

The truth was, our state wasn't doing enough to educate kids. People figured students could drop out and still get a job on a farm or in a factory and make a living wage. The dropout rate was even worse for African-American children.

It is a shameful part of our history that North Carolina and other Southern states fought so hard and so long to avoid giving minority children an education. Their policy, if you can call it that, was outright neglect.

I'm not talking about ancient history here. It was when I was a teenager in high school, and a lot of people in our state remember how it was.

So I look at where we were at a relatively recent time—in 1960. And I look ahead to where I believe we should be in 2010—fifty years after Terry Sanford was elected Governor. I know how the world is changing, because I've seen it change. I've seen our competition all over the world. I know the kind of education our children and grandchildren will need if they are going to compete. And I know we will never give them the education they deserve unless we now set a truly audacious goal.

But it's been forty years since Terry Sanford talked about "quality education," and ever since people have been trying to figure out what to do with our schools. People have always been looking for a silver bullet, one thing that will magically make the schools better. One group says just improve discipline. Another group says just raise teachers' salaries. Another says just put computers in the classroom.

A lot of the silver bullets come from politicians. Too many of them run for office on instant solutions. Educators sometimes go to the opposite extreme. They want to make it complex: long lists of things to do, lists running out your ears. I believe the educators make it too complicated and the politicians make it too simple. They are both wrong.

It dawned on me that our thinking—and my own thinking—had not been focused enough. We had not been clear about what "quality" really is. Obviously, quality meant better, but how much better, and what specific things did we need to do to get better? We didn't measure our progress rigorously, and we didn't report to the public.

Through the years, North Carolina would have a period of progress in education, and then we would fall back. We'd have a spurt forward, and then we'd sit back and think we'd done enough for a while. We've been up and down, starting and stopping—going fast, slowing down. You don't ever get to be number one that way. What would happen if Duke, Carolina, or State skipped recruiting basketball players every other year?

I saw this up-and-down pattern during my own terms as Governor, especially the first terms. We made some progress, but we weren't pursuing better education in a disciplined way with full accountability to the people.

Today, we need a more focused and comprehensive strategy. We need to be very specific about where we are trying to go. We need to realize it's not enough to do just a little more. And we must continue being committed to our goals.

This is the reason I am challenging North Carolinians to commit themselves to making our schools first in America by the end of the first decade of the twenty-first century. Making such a commitment is a way to fix our sights on the future. It's a way to keep our eyes on the prize. It's a way to leave behind the shortcomings and shortsightedness that have held us back in the past. It's a way to build our economy. It's a way to give our children and grandchildren the hopes and opportunities we want them to have.

But it's not enough to simply make a commitment like this one—big as it is, important as it is, and ambitious as it is. We need a plan to get there, a road map to guide us.

So after I set out the challenge in my 1999 State of the State Address, I went to North Carolina's Education Cabinet, which is chaired by the Governor and includes the Superintendent of Public Instruction, the Chairman of the State Board of Education, the President of the University of North Carolina, the President of the Community Colleges, and the President of the State Association of Independent Colleges and Universities. I asked these leaders first to commit themselves and their systems to meeting this challenge over the next ten years. I asked them to spell out *exactly* what number one in America means and how we get there.

We came up with five goals that we have to reach to make our schools the best in America:

Goal 1: A Smart Start. Every child must start school healthy and ready to learn. That's what the early-childhood initiative we call Smart Start is all about.

Goal 2: Excellent Teaching. Every student must have a good teacher every year, and every school must have a good principal.

Goal 3: Safe Schools. Schools must be safe, orderly, and caring places. Students can't learn in schools where they're afraid. That's an important part of making schools successful and helping children to learn.

Goal 4: High Student Performance. We must have high expectations and high standards for student performance. This means setting out specifically what students need to know and be able to do in order to be successful. Our expectation is that *every student* will learn that much and more. If we don't expect them to learn, they won't. If we do expect students to learn and if we put in the resources that are necessary, they will learn.

Goal 5: Community Support. The schools must have strong support from parents, the community as a whole, and business people. And every child who needs extra help from a mentor should have one.

So these are the five big goals we set. And to be first in America, we must reach all five of them. It's like a good football team. It takes all the parts working together: a good coaching staff, an offensive line, a good quarterback, running backs, and receivers. It takes a defensive line, linebackers, and defensive backs. It takes special teams. The great football teams are strong at every position every year, and that's the same approach we ought to take to educating our children.

There's something else that is critically important: We have to measure how we're doing. We have to look at what's working, where we are, and in what direction we are headed. We can't just snap our fingers and jump to number one. We have to work day after day after day until we get there.

I have friends who run marathons. Going for first in America is a marathon, not a sprint. They work on their running every day. They work hard. They have to know how they're doing and keep track of their times. In the same way, we need to see progress in our schools. It's not enough to say that ten years from now we *hope* to be number one. We have to see what we're doing every year, set new goals every year, and keep pushing harder at each step until we get there.

This is where we came up with the idea of an annual report card to show what number one is: what is best, and who is best. What are the top ten states? Where are we in these rankings? Which direction are we headed? In 2000, for the first time, North Carolina issued a thorough and comprehensive report card that measures—in an objective and honest way—where we are in all five areas. This gives us a yardstick to measure our progress every year to the end of the decade.

Once we know where we stand, we can figure out what it will take to move us in the right direction—what the Governor's program has to be, what the legislature needs to do, what boards of education need to do, and what communities and businesses need to do.

Ultimately, I think we need not just a report card for our schools statewide, but a report card for each school, so parents and citizens will know how their own schools are doing.

This must be a public endeavor. It must all be done out in the open, and people have to know how we're doing. If we're not doing as well as we should, we have to say so. We have to be completely open and honest and frank about our progress.

So, we have set out a truly audacious challenge for North Carolina: to be first in America in education by 2010. We have set out the five specific goals we must meet. Now let's take a closer look at how we achieve each one.

CHAPTER 3

Goal 1. *A Smart Start*

THERE USED TO BE A FEELING—in fact, I used to feel this way—that if we just worked hard enough at improving the schools, we could help every child learn. If they didn't learn, we just hadn't tried hard enough or provided enough resources. It turns out that's not true. Things happen in the earliest years of children's development that are absolutely essential if they are to learn later on. If those good things don't happen for children, we cannot make up for them later. No matter how we try, no matter how much money we spend, we cannot do it.

I was slow to grasp this fundamental fact myself, but my wife, Carolyn, knew it, and she got me to see the light when our grandchildren were born. I began to sense how much was going on in my grandchildren's minds when I held them, talked to them, and played with them. I thought I could see something happening in the way they would respond, look at me, and listen. It's almost as if I could see them beginning to learn.

Then Carl Sagan spoke at an Emerging Issues Forum at North Carolina State in 1990. I read his book about the evolution of human beings, about the early stages of development and how critical they are. A number of new scientific studies reported on brain development. For the first time, many of us learned that every child is born with an incredible number of brain cells—billions of them. Intelligence develops and babies learn to talk, see, feel, and move as the cells become connected by tiny neurons. These connections happen when children are stimulated, when they hear new sounds, see new colors, and feel new shapes, and when they're touched by caring adults. Over time, as all these things happen, the little brain gets "wired up." A child develops intelligence and the ability to exercise mental functions.

If a child doesn't get those experiences, if she's neglected or left lying in a crib with no one to hold her and love her, these connections don't happen. She doesn't fully develop the ability to think and learn. No matter what happens later in her life, the necessary connections can never happen to the extent they could have and should have happened in her earliest years.

As I studied this matter further, I realized we'd been missing the boat. We thought we could fix kids later on, but we cannot. We have to get it right from the very beginning.

That means we have to do three things: first, provide good health care; second, provide good child care, in homes and in child care centers; and third, work with parents so they can help their own children develop and thrive.

I was struck by how many children don't get the care they need. My own grandchildren were doing fine, but not every child was. I remember going by a shack near my farm, and I kept seeing this little child there. It was the middle of the winter, but he wasn't wearing anything but a diaper. He was wandering aimlessly on the front porch, and he was holding a bottle, always empty, trying to suck out one last drop of milk. He looked malnourished. He was certainly cold. I never once saw an adult come out for that child, wrap him up in warm clothes, and take him back inside. In my mind, that child became the poster child for Smart Start.

Smart Start was the name we gave our early-childhood initiative, an approach that was a first for the nation, something new and unlike any other state effort. It has caught people's imagination and inspired similar initiatives throughout the country. It's the main reason that, in 2000, *Working Mother* magazine ranked North Carolina as one of the top states in its commitment to young children and described North Carolina as "among the most creative and resourceful states in America when it comes to child care."

Smart Start grew out of my feeling that we shouldn't follow the normal big-government approach: putting all children in child care centers run by the state. It seemed to me that the state had problems enough handling K–12. We were a long way from getting that right. We sure couldn't put the added responsibility for child care on the schools.

There was an alternative. Carolyn had chaired the board of the child care center at the Wilson Presbyterian Church. Our children had gone to very good church-run centers. So it struck me that, yes, we had to provide better child care and other services, but instead of government running it all, we should put local people in charge.

What developed in my mind was a vision of a public-private partnership within each county, where we would bring together all the people who have an interest in children—parents, educators, health professionals, employers, church people, and others—to be in charge of their own local early-childhood initiative. I consciously stayed away from the word "program" because I don't want it to be a "government program." The money does come from the government by and large, and the state has a responsibility to make sure that there's good early-childhood development. But Smart Start needs to be a locally based, community-based effort.

I recruited a Raleigh businessman, Jim Goodmon, to be the first chairman of the statewide Smart Start board, the North Carolina Partnership for Children. He believes passionately in helping young children, and he understands the importance of local involvement and business involvement. He helped persuade the legislature to establish Smart Start, and he persuaded business people to support it financially. He also put the substantial resources of his company, one of North Carolina's largest broadcasters, behind the concept.

The secret of Smart Start is that it belongs to the local people. It's theirs, and they own it. It's doing great things for children, and it has matured as a new kind of system to help children during the early years. We now have partnerships covering all one hundred counties. We have trained the boards of directors in what good care and development of children mean, and they have made enormous progress in setting aside turf battles and working together for the kids.

Since Smart Start's inception, almost 49,000 new child care spaces have been provided and more than 295,000 children have received higher-quality care. Child care subsidies have been provided to the families of over 132,000 children, enabling their parents to work. Over 158,000 parents have received parenting and health education. And more than 297,000 children have received early intervention and preventive health care services, such as dental, vision, hearing, and developmental screenings.

But we still have a long way to go. Many of the partnerships only recently got most of their money. We still have places where there are not enough child care spaces, particularly for infants and toddlers. There aren't enough spaces for the children of second- and third-shift workers. We don't have enough high-quality centers. Too many children are still getting custodial care. We don't have nearly enough good teachers.

Quality early-childhood education requires well-qualified teachers. They have to understand about children, understand how to teach them, and know how to work with them, encourage them, and stimulate them. That takes training and knowledge.

In the public schools, we're focusing on high standards for teachers and raising pay dramatically. We've raised the average public school teacher's salary to $42,000 a year. We haven't begun to do that much for early childhood. Average salaries for early-childhood teachers are less than half of those for public school teachers. How does that make sense? The earliest years are the most important and most formative years. How can we justify paying those teachers less? Some of them hardly make a living wage. Teachers in early childhood should be on the same salary schedule as public school teachers.

We also need the right kind of employment and family-leave policies for parents who need to take care of children. The truth is that we will never be able to do enough through Smart Start or through government. It takes parents teaching their children, helping them develop in the right way, and spending enough time with them. Many people need a lot of help in learning to be good and effective parents.

Of course, good health care is also essential for a good start in life. The earliest years are the time to spot vision, hearing, and developmental problems. We have a much better chance to correct them then. Immunization and regular checkups by a doctor are a must. We are providing better health care for many children; our child health insurance program is the best in the nation. But we still have a long way to go.

So I'm not just interested in selling people on Smart Start, as good as it is. I want people to understand about the earliest years and what has to happen in them. We need to see early childhood as an *education* issue. I made my commitment to Smart Start not just because I love kids, though I do, but because it is essential for schools to work and for children to learn. Our goal is to have every child start school on day one, healthy and ready to learn. I like to say "ready to fly."

CHAPTER 4

Goal 2. *Excellent Teaching*

I'VE ALWAYS HAD A DEEP RESPECT for teachers. I saw in my mother what excellent teaching was, and I had some great teachers.

My first-grade teacher was Miss Taylor. She loved every child in her room. She was good at helping us all get started and finding different ways to reach us. We all came out of first grade learning.

I had a wonderful teacher in the fifth grade, Miss Smith, who was a real disciplinarian. She was really tough on me. I was inclined to talk a lot. When I finished my work, she wouldn't let me talk. I had to fill the time, so I started reading; in the fifth grade, I read every book written by Zane Grey. Since I wasn't allowed to talk, all I could do was pull out a book and read it. I came to love reading, and that, of course, has served me pretty well.

Miss Wainwright was my English teacher in high school. She was a tough old bird who dyed her hair blue. She didn't mean to dye it blue, but she did. Behind her back, we called her the Blue Goose. But, let me tell you, she taught me grammar. She made us believe it was a mortal sin not to have agreement between your subject and verb. Even now I wince when people get this wrong.

Then I had Coach Cockrell, my history teacher, who was also my football and basketball coach. He'd pace around the room and get all excited about battles. We didn't get so excited about the battles, but we were excited about the "Coach." We learned our history so we wouldn't let *him* down. In fact, I began to like history, and maybe that's where I started toward my life in politics and public service.

Then there was Mr. Sheffield, my vocational agriculture teacher. He was a strong, tough guy. He'd grown up poor as he could be. But he'd gone to State and graduated in his mid-thirties. He got me interested in the Future Farmers of America, a farm youth organization with training and contests in parliamentary procedure and public speaking. I loved it. I was beginning to get a glimpse into a future that might be right for me. Mr. Sheffield had high goals for us. He really expected us to do well. He demanded it.

There was a great thing about his teaching, and I've reflected on it many times. We had these two brothers in my class who had never learned to read. Here we were in high school, in the eleventh grade, and they didn't know how to read. But they were two of the best bear hunters, deer hunters, raccoon hunters in eastern North Carolina. They had fine hunting dogs. So Mr. Sheffield would begin his class with a little discussion about hunting and dogs. He'd get those boys engaged in the discussion, and then he'd gradually shift it over to the lesson topic of the day, say "soils." I don't know how he got from bear hunting to soils, but he did. And he kept those boys interested—and learning.

He watched every student every second. If he saw our minds wandering, he'd pull us back into the discussion. He was a master, just like an orchestra leader, watching every instrument, knowing when each one is supposed to come in, getting the best out of each one. That's what a great teacher does.

I don't want to romanticize those days, but in some ways it was easier to have a great teacher then. A lot of the people who might once have gone into teaching now have other opportunities. Years ago, women had three career choices: secretary, nurse, or teacher. The schools don't have that monopoly on women anymore.

Our schools started having to compete in the marketplace for good teachers, and they weren't prepared to do it. At the same time, the job of teaching got harder. The knowledge and skills that students need to learn kept going up. The support and help that many students got from busy parents, or single parents, kept going down. The gap had to be filled by the schools.

Teaching became more complex. Imagine you're a teacher, with twenty-five, thirty, or even more students in your class, all from different backgrounds and with different levels of knowledge, all learning in different ways and requiring different teaching techniques. In fact, many of them speak different languages. You have to know a great deal about your subject matter, and new knowledge is coming out all the time. You have to keep all the students learning and moving along together, although one or two of them may be way behind and hold up the whole class. That's what teachers face every day!

I learned about these problems from the best teachers in America. After my first two terms as Governor, the Carnegie Corporation in New York asked me to lead an effort to raise standards for teachers and make teaching a more respected profession in our nation. I ended up helping to found the National Board for Professional Teaching Standards.

In my ten years as chairman of that board, I spent thousands of hours listening to America's best teachers talk about their teaching. They spelled out what accomplished teachers need to know and do. We used what we learned to establish a nationwide system of standards for teachers and "board-certify" those who meet high standards. Our system is similar to the way doctors are board-certified in their specialties, and it's just as rigorous.

I came to understand and appreciate what is required for excellence in teaching and what excellent teachers can accomplish. What became clear to me was this: If we can get the right kind of teachers and give them the support they need to teach successfully, the students will learn. The key is the *teacher*. It isn't the building, or technology, or even discipline—though they are all necessary. If you have a teacher who really grabs you, like "Herr" Watts, who taught world literature to my son and daughter at Broughton High School in Raleigh, that experience will inspire you and get you excited about your own possibilities. When the right teacher lights a spark, all of a sudden you get interested in some area. You start following up. You start reading about it. You might decide you want to work in that field or go to college and study more. That's what great teachers can do for you.

The National Board for Professional Teaching Standards has had a profound impact in creating a true profession of teaching. Here is what the board says the best teachers must know and be able to do:

First of all, they have to really *care about children* and be committed to every child's education. There's a quality of caring that they have to possess. They have to get to know every child and his family and make sure every child is learning.

Second, they have to *know their subject matter* very well,

and they have to know how to teach it to every child. Different children learn in different ways. Teachers have to connect with every child, bring to life the subject they're teaching, and make it relevant to their students' lives.

Third, teachers have to know how to *manage and monitor student learning*. They have to be able to lead a class, maintain discipline, assess how well children are doing, and know if students are learning. If they aren't learning, the teacher has to figure out what is wrong and how to correct it.

Fourth, teachers have to *continue to learn* and to *think constantly* about how to improve their teaching. There is more knowledge and more research coming out all the time, and we're learning more about good teaching all the time. The new information may be about the subject they teach, or it may be about child development and how kids learn. Teachers have to stay up to date and study constantly, just as a lawyer has to read new decisions from the Supreme Court and a surgeon has to learn new operating techniques. And teachers have to examine how new information can help the students in their classes learn more.

Fifth, they have to be members of what we call *learning communities*. They have to work constantly with their colleagues. They have to talk with each other about their students: how are they doing in your class, what problems are you seeing, how can we work together? How can the English teacher and the history teacher work together on writing skills? How can the science and math teachers work together on problem-solving skills? What difficulties are the counselors finding with these kids? Everybody has to be part of a team that works with all children and with their families and with the community. It's an enormous job.

What I've learned about teaching—and the ideas I had developed about a good start for every child—motivated me to run for Governor again in 1992. It was clear to me, as never before, what it would take to make schools excellent. Not just how to talk about the problem, and not a silver bullet to magically solve it. But how to do the job. And it all started with a smart start and an excellent teacher for every child.

Then, in 1994, I was asked to chair the National Commission on Teaching and America's Future, a bipartisan group of business and education leaders, governors, teachers, and school administrators. We came up with a blueprint for getting better teachers in America's schools—recruiting them, preparing them, and supporting them. We said there ought to be a new civil right in America: the right of every child to have a competent, caring, and qualified teacher in every class every year.

All these experiences came together when I ran for Governor a fourth time in 1996. I promised in my campaign that we would do two things: raise standards for our teachers so that every student would have a good one, and raise teachers' pay to the national average in the next four years. A lot of people said we couldn't do it. Heck, we'd slipped to forty-third among the states in the salaries we paid our teachers. The media was startled by my proposal. They said, "Governor, do you know that will cost a billion dollars?" I said, "Yes I do, and good teachers are worth every penny of it."

And we did it. We're now at the national average for the first time in our history. In 1999 we ranked twenty-third, and when the 2000–2001 figures come out we should be in the top twenty. We raised the average teacher salary from $31,000 to $42,000 in just four years. I doubt that any state has ever done it as quickly. For teachers in the first several years of their careers—years when we lose so many to other jobs—salaries went up nearly 50 percent. By the end of 2000, 2,389 of our teachers had achieved National Board Certification. That is more than in any other state and one-fourth of all the board-certified teachers in America. Our Legislature encourages teachers to become board-certified by paying them an extra 12 percent salary each year. Teachers can also earn bonuses under our testing program and can earn extra pay for being mentors to new teachers.

Along with raising teacher pay, we passed a landmark piece of legislation in 1997, the Excellent Schools Act. It raised standards for teachers and tied their salaries to performance and to proof of excellence, such as National Board Certification. It made it easier to get rid of poor teachers.

Our efforts to improve teaching in our schools cannot slow down. We must continue to improve standards, to do more professional development, and to weed out poor teachers. We must continue to raise pay. Teaching must become comparable in pay to jobs that are luring away many of our best teachers. Under our present pay schedules, top teachers who teach for thirty years and have a master's degree and National Board Certification can make over $60,000 a year. By the end of this decade, that should be up to $100,000 a year. If we raise teachers' salaries and benefits and treat them like professionals, we will attract and keep more good teachers. A big part of our strategy to have enough good teachers is to *retain* those we already have.

We should remember that good teachers don't teach just for pay. They need to be respected and treated like professionals. Like all of us, they want to be appreciated. Why don't we give our teachers the same kind of support we give our ministers? After church on Sunday, when I shake hands with my minister, I always thank him for his sermon and tell him how much Carolyn and I appreciate him. We should do the same thing every time we see our children's teachers.

Another challenge is to develop many more good teachers. In North Carolina we face a serious shortage of qualified teachers in certain fields. That's especially true in areas like science, math, and helping exceptional children. Estimates are that we'll need 80,000 new teachers in our state in the next decade. That's as many *new* teachers as we have *total* teachers today!

It is essential that our public universities and private colleges put a higher priority on solving this problem. They'll have to double the number of new teachers they are preparing, both undergraduates and mid-career professionals who decide they want to become teachers. We know that many School of Education graduates never go into teaching. Of those who do, almost a third leave within the first three years. In some urban areas, *half* of the new teachers quit within five years.

The teaching force in our schools also needs to include role models for all students. In particular, we need more male teachers and more minorities, especially African-Americans and Hispanics.

One of the greatest challenges we face is to get more good teachers into poor schools. Studies have shown that poor and low-performing schools often have less competent teachers and that new, inexperienced teachers are more often assigned to them. This must stop.

Superintendents and school boards need to be committed to turning around poor schools. Little is gained by just reassigning top teachers to poor schools, although superintendents should have the guts to do this sometimes as part of the solution. We must make these hard-to-staff schools more attractive to teachers. Three things would help: putting in a top-flight principal, focusing on good facilities and support for teachers, and paying bonuses—big bonuses—to teachers who teach in these schools.

New York City offered a 15 percent bonus to teachers who volunteered to teach in its lowest-performing schools. Few accepted. School officials there now believe it will take a $20,000-a-year pay differential to attract high-quality teachers to the most difficult places, and I believe they're about right. In North Carolina, we had forty-three low-performing schools in the 1999–2000 school year, including charter schools. If we decided to take a fresh start and pick a faculty in each of these schools to turn them around, and if we committed to pay each of these teachers an extra $10,000 or $20,000 a year, I think we'd see miracles happen.

It would be a big step toward making our state first in America. We'd send a signal that we're committed to making every school good and to helping every child learn. Many parents who feel their children are trapped in poor schools would be ecstatic.

While good teachers are the most important ingredient in successful schools, getting them and keeping them will require good principals.

The principal is the CEO of the school. He or she (and more and more are women who've been excellent teachers) must have high ambitions for the school, inspire and support the faculty, scour the state for good teachers to hire, enforce discipline, and constantly focus on achievement and success for every student. She must invite and welcome parental and community participation and involve the whole school team in setting goals and devising strategies for success.

Just as the school board's main responsibility is to hire and support a good superintendent, the superintendent's chief job is selecting good principals and helping them get and keep good teachers.

This is a particular challenge for low-performing schools, but it can be done—if we're willing to make changes. First, we must resolve in every county that we will not tolerate failing schools. Whatever it takes, we are going to turn them around. "School assistance teams" sent out by the State Board of Education and the State Superintendent of Public Instruction are already having success that is achieving national attention. But we must do more.

My idea is to put the best principals in the worst schools.

This would signal to the community that we're serious about helping all schools succeed. It would spur us to focus immediately on finding more good principals.

But getting top principals to go to failing schools will not be easy. It will take three things: giving the principals freedom to select their faculties, giving them flexibility in using their schools' funds as long as their academic performance is good, and paying a substantial bonus to principals who go to the poorest schools. We should consider bonuses of $25,000 to $50,000 a year for principals who are carefully selected for their potential to turn around the state's worst schools. They should stay at those schools, with their bonuses continuing, for at least three years. I believe top-flight teachers will volunteer to teach in our lowest-performing schools if the best principals head them—and if the teachers are paid adequately.

North Carolina's progress in improving our schools during the 1990s has shown us what we *can* do. We've made more progress than any other state in America. We are now paying much better salaries and beginning to get and keep good teachers, principals, and other school professionals. The word about career opportunities in our schools is beginning to get out. But it will take a sustained commitment to this goal for the next ten years and beyond to get us to first in America.

As I think about my years studying education and teaching, I realize that what I've come to believe confirms what I first learned from my mother about excellent teaching. Excellent teaching means a commitment to children. It means knowing your subject and how to teach it, being able to manage and monitor a classroom, continuing to learn and develop as a professional, and working with others who can help children succeed.

Most of all, it's believing that *every child* can learn. That's what my mother believed, and it's a basic foundation for what we are trying to do. We can't be first in America without a good teacher for every child and a good principal for every school. With them, we can.

CHAPTER 5

Goal 3. *Safe Schools*

CHILDREN CAN'T LEARN if they don't feel safe in school. They can't study if they're not in orderly classrooms and school buildings. They can't succeed if the schools don't have good teachers who know them and care about them and teach them. So we need to pay more attention to the kind of schools we have.

The way to look at this is to ask: What do I want for *my* child? That's always the test. Obviously, we want a clean, well-lit, well-equipped building. Classes should be orderly. There should be a caring, nurturing atmosphere. The students aren't numbers; they're individuals. They are our children—every one of them is precious to us. We send them off to school in the morning in a good mood and with high hopes for the day. We want people to take good care of them, the same way we would.

Most of all, we want them to be safe when they're at school. We want them to come home to us safe, having had a good experience, excited about what they did—not crying, scared, or traumatized.

Violence in the schools is something that we absolutely should not tolerate. It's bad enough to have crime on the street, but we must not have it in our schools. Yes, a fight will break out once in a while in the course of things and people can get hurt playing football and other sports, but this business of having guns, drugs, and knives and young criminals in the schools committing violence is intolerable. We should not accept it, and we *can* put an end to it.

If violence is a problem, we must do whatever it takes to change it. *Whatever it takes.* Whether it takes uniformed officers, metal detectors, searching lockers, or searching cars, we must keep students safe.

Unfortunately, children in America today are exposed to too much violence from an early age. The typical child spends more time watching television than going to school, has less contact with adults, especially during the after-school hours when problems are most likely to occur, and gets mixed messages from society about what's right and what's wrong.

There are other problems: increasing divorce rates, single-parent families, abuse and neglect. More and more children are coming to school with social and psychological problems. We have too many youngsters in the classroom whose early experiences haven't steered them toward becoming good citizens who treat each other right. A lot of violent kids are that way because of where they came from. We hope that in the future we can change things in children's earliest years and they won't have so much trouble getting along. But whatever the cause, we can't tolerate violence in our schools.

When we've got young thugs in a school, we should kick them out. Don't let them stay in that school and hurt our kids. Don't let them prevent other students from learning. But we shouldn't put them on the street. Every student under sixteen should be in school—somewhere. Put disruptive students in an alternative school on a different campus or in a different building.

If your school is having a problem with violence and safety, demand that the principal make the necessary changes—or change him. He is the CEO, and he has no more important responsibility than to make sure kids are safe every single day. Get the county board of education or sheriff's department to put as many uniformed officers in the school as it needs. At some schools, the kids have agreed to searches of their book bags and their lockers and even their cars in the parking lot. They *agreed* to these searches. Now, searches and police officers are not what we normally want in our schools. But whenever there is a problem with violence or disorder, we've got to do whatever it takes to eliminate it.

Modern technology can help make schools safer. At Springfield Middle School in Wilson County, a new school where my grandson goes, the principal can stand in his office and watch a screen that shows live video from twelve security cameras all over the building. He can see every hallway. He can watch every kid changing classes. We can watch out for students that way, or we can do it by simply having enough teachers and parents in the halls, in the bathrooms, and around the lockers.

One of the key issues that I believe affects safety and the whole educational enterprise is the *size* of our schools. This is an area where we have made terrible mistakes in America and in North Carolina. Too many schools are just too big.

I supported consolidation of schools years ago. I went to a school that was first through twelfth grade. But along the way we got this idea that for children to have the maximum opportunities, they needed to be able to take this great variety of courses. Your schools weren't really excellent unless they offered a hundred courses or more. To offer that many courses the schools had to be huge. Since World War II, while the number of schools in the United States has actually declined by 70 percent, the average size of schools has *increased by 50 percent.*

This didn't happen by accident. We planned it. We thought big schools would be more efficient and offer greater opportunities by giving students more choices. But now there's a lot of evidence that we were wrong. These big schools have enormous bureaucracies, and that makes them less efficient. But the worst problem is that too many kids get lost in the crowd. They fall through the cracks. Of course, there are high achievers who get involved in activities and do well, but a lot of youngsters don't feel cared for and don't get much personal attention. They're just walking the halls, going to class, unknown, just faces in the crowd.

Every student ought to have an environment like the one at Emma Conn School, just a few blocks from the Governor's Mansion in Raleigh. Virginia Cardenas is a marvelous principal who literally knows every child in the school. She's at the front door at the end of school saying goodbye to every child. All of them are loved and cared for. The teachers and the school staff value every one of them. They keep tabs on them, too. Those kids won't fall through the cracks—not one of them.

That's the way it ought to be, and that's why I believe no high school should have more than one thousand students, no middle school more than six hundred, and no elementary school more than four hundred.

Vice President Al Gore got it right with a statement he made during the 2000 presidential campaign. He said: "We've done some things wrong in education, and here's one of them: herding all students in a twenty-five-mile area into overcrowded factory-style high schools. When teachers and principals must practice crowd control, it becomes impossible to spot the early warning signs of violence, depression, or academic failure—and it becomes even harder to do something about it."

This is one lesson from Columbine High School in Colorado. It was in a tremendously fast-growing area, a high school of nearly two thousand students. It was a fine building, but it had way too many kids, including some alienated boys who organized a "Trench Coat Mafia." One day, two of these boys brought guns and bombs to school under their trench coats, and nobody knew it. We should be outraged at the very idea of having a school where kids are this alienated and this violent—and nobody knows it. These young people became more and more alienated and further and further out there in a violent fantasy world. Then all of a sudden the dam burst; they brought in their guns and bombs, and innocent children and adults died. It didn't have to happen.

We need to do something radical about school size in North Carolina. First, we shouldn't build any more big schools. And we should take this step now, while the student population is growing and many counties are building new schools. Let's make them smaller. Second, we should immediately begin converting these huge schools into moderate-size, effective schools, even small schools. Break them apart. Make schools within schools. Take a high school of two thousand students and divide it into two schools. Organize it so you have two principals and two sets of faculty. Maybe they can share some of the present facilities like auditoriums, gyms, and athletic fields. But make schools a manageable size so that every student in a school is known, cared for, and encouraged to participate. Every student should feel a part of the school.

We can do this. If you want smaller schools, you should demand them. Go to the school board and tell them you want smaller schools. Tell them you don't think your kids are safe and adequately cared for in big schools, and you want things changed. They are *your* schools. They don't belong to the school board or the county commissioners. They belong to the people.

We should take the same attitude about class size. If you want smaller classes, let the politicians know—and be willing to pay the price. Reducing class size does make a difference. But research shows that it takes a *dramatic* reduction in class size—down to as few as fifteen or sixteen students per class—to make a real difference. That will cost a lot of money. Perhaps we should begin by taking this step in the early grades and in low-performing middle schools and high schools.

The important idea here is knowing the students, staying up with them, and seeing that they are learning and being treated right. We need to be tending to their emotional needs. We know what happens when they get into middle school and high school: their hormones are raging and they're up and down every day. We can remember being that age. They need care and love. They may be hard to get along with, but our job is to get along with them and help them.

I believe strongly in having school resource officers, uniformed law officers, in every middle school and high school, and I've put money in my budgets to do it. But if we make schools the right size, organize them right, and have enough people around to pay attention to every kid, we won't need so many uniformed officers, surveillance cameras, and locker searches.

Actually, we've made some real progress in making schools safer in North Carolina. When I began my third term as Governor in 1993, I found we had serious problems with school violence. We went after it aggressively. I appointed a Task Force on School Violence, and we passed some tough laws—especially laws against bringing weapons to school. We sent a signal that our schools wouldn't tolerate trouble. We set up a statewide Center for the Prevention of School Violence to work with the schools and share successful strategies. Since 1993 there's been a 21 percent decline in the number of incidents of school violence reported in North Carolina, and the number of guns found in the schools has gone down 68 percent.

The hours right after school and before parents get home from work are a time when we need to pay special attention to the safety and activities of students. Many elementary schools provide after-school care for students who need it during those hours. But very few middle schools do. Yet the middle-school years are the years when kids start to look for trouble, and afternoons are when they find it. I'd like to see every middle school *required* to provide an after-school program. If the school system cannot finance such a program, parents at least should have the opportunity to sign up their children for a fee. And it should be free for students whose parents cannot afford it.

During the special crime session of the legislature that I called in 1994, we established the SOS (Support Our Students) program to provide safe places for some middle-school students who especially need this kind of help. There are other good programs like "Communities in Schools." But we're meeting only a small portion of the need. I'd like to see all communities in North Carolina reaching out and helping their kids who need care and protection after school.

Students need to be taught well, but many of them need extra help, more role models, and a level of caring that the basic school program cannot provide. That is the real key to eliminating violence and disorder, and it's imperative if we are going to make our schools first in America.

CHAPTER 6

Goal 4. *High Student Performance*

KATI HAYCOCK OF THE EDUCATION TRUST has some surprising things to say about her discussions with adults and students in school systems across the country where there are large achievement gaps. Typically the adults, including teachers, say that the students in low-performing schools do not achieve because they are from poor families, their parents have little education, and they live in bad neighborhoods. What students say is very different: first, the adults don't believe we can learn, and, second, many of our teachers aren't very good.

The students are right on both counts. The adults did not believe these students could learn, and they did not provide good teachers for them. That was the adults' fault, not the students' fault.

We must understand a fundamental truth: All kids can learn. To help them, we must first determine what students need to learn and be able to do in order to be successful.

What do they need to know to be ready for the next grade? What do they need to know to graduate and to get a good job? Those skills and competencies are the *standards* that we set in our curriculum and teach to students in our public schools.

One of the simplest yet most important things I have learned is this: To have good schools, we must have high standards and high expectations for all schools—and for all children. So a vital element of our effort to make North Carolina schools first in America is setting standards and measuring our progress in achieving them.

I remember visiting Fred L. Wilson Elementary School in Kannapolis, where more than half of the students came from low-income families. They went from having the lowest test scores in the school district to having the highest. They did it by focusing on performance and on how *every child* was doing. They didn't look at averages. They didn't treat students as a group. The teachers and the staff focused on having every child learn at grade level. They got the parents involved, and together they did the job.

We can get children up to grade level in every school in North Carolina. It's not an unrealistic goal; it's what we should expect to happen. And the effort shouldn't stop with graduation from high school. We want students to go to college. Every student who graduates from high school should get at least two years of college or technical training, after which everyone should be able to get a good job with good pay.

I pushed for higher standards during my first two terms as Governor. During the late seventies and early eighties, we put in place the state's first standardized tests and a minimum competency test that was required for high school graduation. But I spent a lot more time thinking about this during the eight years I was out of office, between 1985 and 1993. I was working with a lot of businesses, doing a lot of studying about America's economic position, and traveling to Japan working with business clients.

I had begun to see the need for higher standards in my first terms as Governor, when I was recruiting industry for the state. Many of the first Japanese plants that came to North Carolina started by putting their assembly functions here. They made the valuable components in Japan and sent them here merely for assembly. They were doing the high-value work over there—research, development, and original manufacturing. We were doing the low-value work of putting the parts together.

That clearly had to change, and it would take bright, creative, and highly educated people to change it. In fact, we had already started on the necessary improvements. We had created the Microelectronics Center of North Carolina, started work toward a Biotechnology Center, and established the North Carolina School of Science and Mathematics, which became a national model. We began targeting the emerging high-technology industries that had such a huge potential for good jobs.

But we had just started. We weren't doing enough. We weren't competing successfully, in large measure because we weren't educating our people well enough. There were some management issues involved, but by and large it was a matter of how much employees had learned, how effectively they could perform, and how creative they were in finding new and better ways to do things. Good education and training are what it takes to be successful.

The choice we faced was the subject of a national group on which I served in 1990, the Commission on the Skills of the American Workforce. Its report was titled "America's Choice—High Skills or Low Wages." You have to choose. If you have low skills, you'll have low wages; if you have high skills, high wages. You get paid for the value of your work.

The world economy has changed dramatically over the last two decades. The United States has far less control over world economic events. Capital can move from Charlotte to Hong Kong in seconds, and stock markets are open twenty-four hours a day around the world. Technology cannot be captured and kept; people will buy it or steal it. The only real asset we have is our people. Whether or not they are bright, creative, innovative—that is our key.

Through all of this, one of our biggest problems in education has been focusing too much on inputs, not results. Many educators told us that our progress in education was measured by how much money we spent. They didn't want their performance measured, or teachers' performance, or students' performance. They just wanted more money. Well, I want more money for the schools too. But I want to measure how well we are doing with the money and how much the children are learning.

It's also important to insist that our schools set high, real-world standards for what *all* students should learn, and that teachers teach *all* students to meet the same standards. To assume that students of a particular race or background cannot learn is factually wrong—and morally wrong.

Our efforts to set good standards for North Carolina students started in the eighties when the State Board of Education approved a "standard course of study." In 1993, we established the Education Commission on Standards and Accountability to determine what students need to know and be able to do to graduate and get a good job. The commission had a series of well-attended hearings around the state asking businesses and employers what knowledge and skills were needed in jobs. Then we put in a statewide testing program in grades three, five, and eight and for selected high school courses to measure whether students have learned what they need to know to move on, to be successful in the next grade, and to graduate. We call this our "ABC's program."

We actually measure two different things. First, we assess where the *students* are—whether they are at grade level in their subjects and prepared to move on to the next level and be successful. Second, we measure the progress the *school* is making—whether the students in that school, on average, are making the progress they should be making. Are they mastering a full year's worth of material during the year? Are they making a full year's progress? Not a half year, not eight months, but a full year's worth of progress.

If they make a full year's progress, we say that the school had "expected growth." Teachers in these schools get a $750 bonus. If they exceed a year's growth and achieve 110 percent or more progress, the school is credited with "exemplary growth." Teachers in these schools get a $1,500 bonus.

Our main goal is to have each student in a school learning at grade level. If 80 percent of the students in a school are scoring at grade level, we call it a "School of Distinction." If it's 90 percent *and* the students have shown at least a year's worth of growth, we call it a "School of Excellence." In 2000, 70 percent of our schools achieved either expected growth or exemplary growth. Of 2,115 participating schools, 509 were Schools of Distinction—up from 158 four years before. Seventy-three were Schools of Excellence—up from just 12 four years earlier. So we're seeing good progress in our schools. But we're a long way from where we want to be in terms of all students performing at grade level.

In the spring of 1994, 56 percent of North Carolina students scored at grade level. Six years later, in the spring of 2000, that number had increased to 70 percent. That's one-fourth more students scoring at grade level, in just six years!

But that still leaves 30 percent who are below grade level, 30 percent who haven't mastered what they should know well enough to be promoted to the next grade. The numbers are higher among some of our students. Fifty percent of African-American students scored below grade level, as did 43 percent of Hispanic students. Among whites it was 20 percent. So we've got a lot of work to do.

Beginning in the spring of 2001, North Carolina will phase in requirements that students perform at grade level on third-, fifth-, and eighth-grade tests in order to be promoted and that they pass an exit exam to graduate. This commitment to accountability may be the greatest challenge to us as a state in the decade ahead: ensuring that *all* students are performing at grade level in our schools and eliminating the racial gap that now exists.

This is going to be tough. I'm proud that my home county, Wilson, got ahead of the curve and started enforcing the end-of-grade standards in 2000. In the middle schools, 567 students failed. They were encouraged to go to summer school and then be retested. After summer school, 389 students—14 percent—still did not meet the standards. Now my county and every other county will be under enormous pressure to help these students who are behind to catch up, and to help all their students learn their subjects *before* the end of school.

We must make clear that our goal is not to flunk kids, but to help them learn every day of the year, to never let them fall behind, to find out what their problems are and give them the help they need—*right then*. It may require smaller classes, more one-on-one instruction time, more conferences with students and parents, and mentoring on afternoons and weekends and in summer schools. Maybe we ought to put kids scoring below grade level into classes with no more than ten or twelve students. Just as with discipline, our motto should be "Whatever it takes." We must help every student get up to grade level and keep going.

The stakes are high. What we need is full accountability, and I believe North Carolinians will respond. I saw how the schools can respond when I did my volunteer work one day at a Raleigh middle school. I had been going there all year on Wednesday afternoons to mentor my student in the library. He and I were usually the only two people in there from three to four o'clock. Then, one afternoon when I arrived, the library was filled with kids getting help from the math teacher. The end-of-grade tests were coming up, and all these kids were behind. So teachers were bringing them in and teaching them more, spending more time helping them learn. The school was giving the students more help.

Now, I know some people quarrel with testing. Some say you ought not to measure because it causes too much stress. Others say we end up "teaching the test" at the expense of other parts of the curriculum. Still others say the tests aren't fair because they aren't perfect. Well, the tests *aren't* perfect; we recognize their limitations and we must improve them every year. But the real danger comes if we *don't* do the testing. Without tests, we have no way of knowing which students and which schools are succeeding—and which need additional help. We have historically had a system in which students weren't measured and held accountable. And we know that large numbers of students failed to learn. They slipped through the cracks, dropped out, and faced a limited future.

We as a society failed them. We didn't measure and report. We weren't candid about how things were going. We didn't change the situation. That's dishonest, and it's wrong.

This is why we've done away with social promotions. In the past, too many students were promoted when they had not learned. That was a great disservice to those students. The next year, they were even farther behind. They got frustrated; many became discipline problems and dropped out. That is going to change in North Carolina.

A new approach is necessary if we're going to have good schools and help every child succeed in North Carolina. We must do it in a way that is fair and that gets parents and families involved in giving help to their children. When test results come in, parents should be informed immediately. Davidson County requires that teachers send the scores home within forty-eight hours.

The teachers and the school should have a clear plan and a strategy to help students catch up and get to grade level. At the beginning of each school year, every student's parents should be informed of his or her status, and the student's teachers and parents should *share* a responsibility to provide remedial help throughout the year. A student shouldn't bring home A's and B's all year and then fail the end-of-grade tests. Educators must ensure that the classwork and the tests are lined up accurately.

We have a major public discussion ahead on this issue. We must listen to each other, and we must have the vision and the sheer guts it will take to stay committed to high standards. If we do this right in North Carolina, we will take a huge step forward. We will be on a course to become first in America.

Let's take the same attitude toward all North Carolina students that we take toward our own children. If we demand a lot and if we have high expectations for our children, they will generally be high achievers. If we have low expectations, they will probably be low achievers. If we as a society want high student performance, we must have high expectations and we must set high standards.

CHAPTER 7

Goal 5. *Community Support*

A RETURN TO FUNDAMENTAL PRINCIPLES often helps us solve our toughest problems. Making public schools work—helping every child learn—is the toughest problem we have in our society. The principle we should return to is this: Educators alone can't do the job of educating our children and making our schools first in America.

I believe deeply in having real professionals in our schools, with enough resources to do the job. But they can't do it alone, and they shouldn't. These are our children! And these are the *public* schools—for every child in this democratic society. They belong to us, the citizens. If we figure out a way to make them excellent as we begin this new century, we will truly make this a nation of "liberty and justice for all."

There is another fundamental principle that school people should always keep before them. Most parents love their children and care deeply about how they do in life, including in school. But they may not believe they have the power to help their children much. They may not know what to do. They may themselves have had a bad experience in school, especially if they were victims of racial discrimination. They may feel they're not wanted in the school.

Many of us are more fortunate. As I think back about my schooling, I realize how much my parents had to do with it. My parents were always involved with the school. They were always supportive in every way that you could be. But what I mainly remember is how much they pushed me to do my best.

I was always expected to do my homework thoroughly. When I played basketball and football in high school, even though I might have a night practice or a late game (and sometimes a late date after a late game), when I did come home at night—before I went to sleep—I had to finish my homework. That was always clear.

When our four children were in school, one of us, Carolyn mainly, would always check on their homework assignments. What did you do today? What do you have to do tonight? Can I help you? Of course, we read with them, took them to the library, bought them books, did everything we could to encourage them. We believed their success in school was as much our responsibility as that of their teachers and the principal. The schools are there to help us. We pay our tax money to build buildings and hire professional educators, but the final responsibility to see that our children learn and prepare for life is *ours*. We're their parents.

I'm reminded of an old saying in the rural area where I grew up. When somebody was making excessive demands of another person, that person would sometimes say: "I didn't take you to raise." Well, the public schools didn't take our kids to raise. There are limits to what they can do in 35 hours of school during a 168-hour week.

We should be aware of what a big difference parents can make in children's learning. One national study showed that parent involvement accounts for as much as 90 percent of the difference in student achievement.

There are several ways that we as parents can help our kids learn. We should help them at home, from the time they're born. We should read aloud to them when they're young. My grandchildren can't get enough of that. In the early grades of school, we should still read to them for at least a half hour each night. Only half of all parents say they do that. We should ask about their school, their courses, and their homework. We should help them with homework and projects. We should ask to see their tests—all of them. We should send this message to our children every day: Your education is important—it's the most important thing in our family. We should limit how much television they watch, have them eat breakfast and dinner with the family, and see that they get eight hours of sleep every night.

We should be involved with their teachers and their school. We should know their teachers and communicate with them frequently about how our children are doing. In today's world, we can communicate with teachers by phone, e-mail, or an Internet "chat." We should go to the school for parent-teacher conferences, especially to review report cards, participate in the PTA, and volunteer to help with school activities and mentor children who need special help.

The schools, however, have a responsibility to get parents involved. First of all, they must really *want* parents involved. One of our children was in a school one time that didn't have a PTA, and the principal was determined not to have one. We worked with other parents to organize one anyway. But his attitude really limited our ability to help the school. In another school the PTA was embraced, and the school was bulging with parents on PTA nights.

Teachers should go the extra mile to get to know parents and their students' family situations. When I practice-taught vocational agriculture at Cary High School, one of the requirements to get my ten hours of credits was to visit the home of every one of my students. I wish every homeroom teacher was required to do that today in North Carolina. School boards could make home visits a requirement and provide help with transportation and security if the student lives in a dangerous neighborhood. Teachers would be amazed at how much they'd learn and how much more they could help their students if they had actually been in their home and met the parents, if they constantly had that home situation in their mind's eye.

Schools should also be innovative about how to involve parents. One good way is to have them participate in an activity like bringing a dish for a supper, going to school to see their child perform in the chorus or band, or being present when she receives an award for schoolwork. Some schools do even more. In Gaston County, they send school buses to pick up parents who need transportation to school activities.

Churches and people of faith are frequently the schools' best friends. My own church in Wilson adopts a school, encourages volunteers to mentor there, and at the beginning of the school year, urges members to buy a new book bag for every child who can't afford one. When I had a town meeting at Tarboro High School a few years ago, there were six ministers present participating in the discussion. They had children from their congregations in the school, and they had come to show their support.

Of all the efforts we are making in North Carolina to improve our schools, I believe involving parents and the community has the greatest unrealized potential. Our goal should be to get all students' families involved in the school and in helping *every child* in the school learn. We should expect the parents and the community to pitch in. We should, quite simply, view the public schools as the most important thing happening in our community.

Business people often are the best at stimulating improvement in the schools. They are generally optimistic "can-do" people who know how much they need well-educated, productive workers. Improving the schools literally goes to their bottom line. Plus, they care about young people and are generally very involved with their own children's education.

This was particularly impressed on me once when I was helping persuade a major national company to move its headquarters to Charlotte. The company would bring hundreds of high-paying jobs and move in lots of top executives. Dozens of cities across the nation were bidding to get this prize. But the way this company's site team made their decision was interesting. Before they ever sat down to discuss taxes, labor costs, regulations, or anything else, they looked at the schools. They sent in a team of people who confidentially examined the quality of the public schools for a whole week. After the schools passed muster, they started talking to the chamber of commerce and spent about a week on other issues. They knew that the schools came first.

North Carolina has a great legacy of business support for education. Our universities and community colleges over the years have had powerful support from business people. We need that same support for the public schools.

A prominent business has the necessary resources, including successful executives and employees with the pull to get things done. They're respected and looked up to. When they say we've got to do more to help our schools, politicians respond. When business people get involved, the school people and the board of education understand that this is important and that they had better do their share, especially in communities that are hungry for economic development and jobs.

That's been a big factor in North Carolina's success in the nineties. We have been successful in getting business people involved and building their support for public schools because we've reached out to them, asked for their help, and encouraged them to take the lead. Higher standards for schools, higher pay for teachers, better teachers, more technology: these are all things that business people have championed, to great effect. Their advocacy and support of schools has had a lot of influence in the General Assembly.

We've had powerful support from big businesses in North Carolina. A number of CEOs have personally testified in the General Assembly and lobbied legislators to get them to approve the Excellent Schools Act, raise standards, increase pay for teachers, and support Smart Start. Leaders of North Carolina businesses, large and small, have made it clear that education is their number one priority.

When I was looking for a chairman of the State Board of Education in 1997, I recruited Phil Kirk, the head of North Carolina Citizens for Business and Industry. He is a former schoolteacher, and he's willing to fight for improvements in education, particularly high standards for teachers and students—and for the funding that is essential. He has the ties and connections that can help attract the level of support that our schools need.

It is a matter of saying: Who can get things done here? Who has the power and the connections and personal leadership to support our schools and help us make them excellent? The answer, at both the state level and the individual community level, is business people.

School leaders need to be talking to business people, listening to them, involving them in their communities. Superintendents and principals ought to court the business community just as they do the school boards and the county commissioners. They should get business leaders to help them lobby for support and resources.

We can't just leave it up to teachers and their organizations to advocate for the schools. The North Carolina Association of Educators and administrators' groups shouldn't have to carry the load. Even PTA and parent groups, which need to be much better organized and more powerful in the legislature, are not enough. We need to have the power centers in business and industry step up and make clear what is at stake: the competitive position of their company in the global economy, and thus the jobs of their employees in the community.

Of course, we need to have influential business leaders pushing for the right policies and the right approaches statewide. But the real key is this: What's happening in our own school? Do we see changes there? Fortunately, we do.

Nortel Networks encourages volunteers to use the company's facilities to train teachers in how to use technology in the classroom. DuPont offers a summer science camp in Kinston for employees' children and grandchildren. Lowe's, based in North Wilkesboro, offers an intensive summer internship program, "The Science of Retail," to give college students experience in the business world. IBM sponsors a "Wired for Learning" program in Charlotte and Durham that gives parents on-line access to their children's assignments, lets them communicate with teachers, and gives them information about the standards students are required to meet. Students can use this program to work on assignments outside the classroom and in teams. Teachers can create student projects and exchange ideas with each other about lessons and curriculum.

Chambers of commerce in this state almost invariably have a major focus on education. Many of their members support school bond issues, work with administrators, and have helped us go a long way in improving our schools.

I've always been impressed with what Catalytica does in Greenville. When that company first came to North Carolina, I encouraged the chairman of the board of directors to get his people deeply involved in improving the schools. He did just that. Larry Siegler, a vice president, and his colleagues at the Greenville facility now meet regularly with the district's superintendent, and the company has adopted two schools. Both were low-performing when they were adopted; now both are doing well. Catalytica has given computers to the schools and helped wire them. The company encourages employees to volunteer at the schools and to attend public meetings, where they stand up for the schools, push the school board and county commissioners to do more to support education, and urge other business people to be more involved.

Business people like those at Catalytica want results, and they are entitled to get results. They want young people to learn. They need employees coming into their businesses who have learned the basics, can communicate, have computational skills, understand science and technology, and can work in groups. Our educators, teachers, principals, and superintendents understand that they're educating for society. They're preparing students for citizenship and to be good parents. And they're also preparing them for *jobs*. The people who will hire them know what knowledge and skills their employees will need, and educators should listen to them and respond to them. We should seek out employers, get them to tell us about their needs, and engage them in helping create schools that meet those needs. Our job is not to educate students in a narrow, highly technical way, but to give them a mastery of the basics and teach them how to think critically, compute, and solve problems. Students can later refine their knowledge and develop specific job skills.

School leaders and makers of education policy in North Carolina must keep up with what is going on in the world. In 2000, I made three trips abroad leading international trade missions. Everywhere I went, countries were pushing to improve the skills of their workers and their young people. I'm asked to make the same speech on improving schools to chambers of commerce in Latin America and Asia that I make in North Carolina. When we recruit companies to our state now, the competition is as likely to be Mexico or South Korea as South Carolina or Ohio.

For this reason, we should take a page from the business and industry handbook. Business people use the term "best in world" to describe the top service or production practices in their fields. They compare themselves to all others in the world. We must do the same thing in education. There is a worldwide education test called TIMSS, the Third International Mathematics and Science Study. We should measure our students' performance against it and make the results available to students, parents, and the business community. We should constantly be looking worldwide for the best ways to help students learn.

The hard reality in the world of economic competition—where the jobs will be tomorrow—is not only that countries are competing against other countries, states against states, and companies against companies. It is literally a matter of *each worker* in North Carolina competing against *each worker* in Germany, Brazil, or China. I have been in their factories and seen workers who are sharp and hardworking. If their knowledge, skills, and productivity exceed ours, the big global companies that compete in the international marketplace will invest in those countries and hire their workers instead of ours.

We are fortunate that our business leaders recognize the symbiotic relationship between the economy and our schools. We are learning a great deal about how to improve the productivity of schools from groups like the North Carolina Partnership for Excellence and the North Carolina Business Committee for Education. But we still have a long way to go in many of our 117 school districts before we have the strong partnerships with the business community that can lift up our schools.

Like parents, business leaders need to be welcomed, to be invited to help. But even with all that we've done to work with the business community in North Carolina, I sometimes feel that we are just scratching the surface. If we deepen and expand the business-school partnerships in each community, in every county, working with every school, we can improve our schools dramatically and keep the focus constantly on the high, real-world standards we have to meet. Business people try to be first in their line of business, and they can help our schools be first in America.

This is why a key part of our strategy is getting all these players actively involved in helping. Businesses can help. Communities at large can resolve that their schools will compete in education just as they compete in football and basketball. Parents, most of all, can make a difference. This whole team must be involved for North Carolina to make the big jump forward that we envision over the next decade.

CHAPTER 8

The Rewards of Mentoring

IT DOESN'T TAKE MUCH TIME to make a difference in the life of a student—or the life of a school. Carolyn and I volunteer an hour or two every week with students in Wake County, and we've done that all through the time I've been Governor. Thousands of people across North Carolina volunteer a lot more time than that in the schools, even if they don't have children there.

The fact is that we have lots of students who need something extra. Remember: Our goal is not just to *teach* students, it's to have them *learn*. Each day they need to learn what it takes to move on to the next day. We should never let one get behind. A lot of children need more time to learn, and they need more personal attention than their teacher can give them, even with good teachers and even if you reduce the teacher-student ratio.

I remember visiting Walter Williams High School in Burlington. We had a town meeting in the library, and I sat beside a student leader who was the quarterback of the state champion football team. I asked him, "What does it take, what do you need, so that you can learn better?" He said, "I need more time. Sometimes I don't get it during the hour that we're in that class; I just need more time." He was willing to work harder and to spend more time on schoolwork, but we had to provide more time for him to learn. Mentoring can do that.

Young people need to be encouraged, to be supported, to feel special. That's what we do with our own kids. We boost them up; we make them feel good. When I mentor a student, one of the first things I do is find out about his life. What does he like, what does he do, what are his interests? What are his favorite pro and college teams? I work with him on homework, but I also try to help pick him up and make him feel better about himself.

If we are successful in our lives and careers, our sons and daughters believe they are going to succeed too. They see how we do it. We encourage and support them. We get them the books and games and everything else they need to help them. We help them get into clubs and activities or play team sports. We put up a basketball net at home so they can practice, and we practice with them. Our kids are in every club and activity you can name; their moms seem to run full-time carpools.

Most of all, we give them our attention, our love, our

help, our encouragement. We make them believe they can succeed. They think: I can do it, I can be successful.

Every young person should feel that way. They should believe that the future is for them too, not just for those well-to-do kids with the best clothes. Getting involved at school in sports, art, music, and other activities gives them a glimpse into the world beyond their own neighborhoods. They get to participate, to succeed.

I started volunteering because my wife did it, and I had seen how valuable it was—how much it helped the students. One year she volunteered almost full-time, because one of our children had a teacher who was not effective.

I volunteered in the programs that I pushed as Governor. My first year as Governor, when we put in the Primary Reading Program, I went to Emma Conn School and volunteered to help first-graders who were behind. I went every week. We read together—they read, I read. I helped them learn to read.

Later on, we put in a minimum competency test that students had to pass to graduate from high school. The first time we gave it, 15 percent of the students flunked. I went on statewide television, reported the results, and urged people to become mentors for low-achieving students.

I went to Broughton High School as a mentor and worked with a wonderful teacher from Australia who taught math. She had a math remedial lab, and I worked with students in the eleventh grade who had failed the test. I did that for two years, at least an hour every week. A lot of people say the eleventh grade is too late to learn, but they're wrong. Students can learn that late, even if they haven't learned up to then. But it takes a lot of individual attention.

Later I worked in a dropout prevention program. For two years I went to Broughton, reported to the counselor's office, and worked with students who were at risk of dropping out.

I remember one of those students so well. She just wouldn't come to school on time; she just couldn't make it. I found out why: her mother was an alcoholic. In the morning, her mother would be lying in bed with a hangover. This girl would get up and get a little brother or sister dressed, out the door, and onto the school bus. Then she'd get the baby dressed and take the baby to a child care center. Finally, she'd get to school herself. Well, we should have been giving her a medal for coming, not griping about her being late. I pled her case and got her classes changed around so she wouldn't miss things.

A lot of these young people don't have an advocate to plead their case. One of the things we do for our own children is intercede for them. Among other things, we help them get jobs. Well, lots of kids don't have that kind of help. They haven't the slightest idea how to get a job, and they don't have the confidence they can get one.

One of the students I was mentoring needed a job, but he didn't know how to get one. He wanted to work at McDonald's. So one night at the Governor's Mansion I called up the McDonald's near where he lived. I asked to speak to the manager, the manager came on, and I said: "This is Governor Hunt. I'm mentoring this young man who wants a job, and I want to ask you if you'd be willing to let him come in and have a job interview." The fellow didn't say much, but I talked to him until I thought I had a job interview set up. Then he turns around and calls the mansion and asks, "Did Governor Hunt really just call me here?" He didn't believe it was the Governor. Anyhow, the student got the job.

Working as a mentor, I found out that students with problems do pretty well in elementary school, but then they get to middle school. That's when you start losing them. That's when you really need to be on top of their situations.

One of the youngsters I mentored in middle school had an especially tough situation. His parents were separated, and he lived with his father in Raleigh. His mother lived over a hundred miles away. His father worked two full-time jobs. He left at seven in the morning, dropped his son off at school, and got home about one or two the next morning. On weekdays the young man never saw his father except at breakfast and on the way to school. Just before the end of the year, they moved to another school district.

I certainly didn't want that young man to change schools one month before the end of the year. I went to the principal and told him about the situation. I asked: Is there a bus that goes by his new home, or can you send a cab for him? What can we do to keep him coming to school here? His father couldn't bring him that far and still get to work on time. We got something worked out, because somebody intervened for him. Most students don't know how to do it for themselves. Sometimes parents aren't motivated enough to do it, and many of them feel powerless. Intervening for students is one really helpful thing that mentors can do.

Mentoring can be a great personal experience. It's been rewarding to hear from students I've worked with over the years, how they've been successful in their lives and how much they appreciated someone showing an interest in them, how it had given them a little extra encouragement and spark to be successful. One of them told me that I kept him from dropping out of school. But I always got back far more from them than I gave.

So, yes, we have to have a good teacher for every child, but we also need a good *mentor* for every child who is at risk—academically or socially. We really need that, and nothing less than that. And our communities can provide it.

There is no substitute for a loving parent, but not every child gets guidance and encouragement at home. Sometimes parents are doing a good job, but their children still need extra help and attention. Young people with mentors are more likely to get good grades and have good relationships with their peers and with adults. They're less likely to skip school, less likely to use drugs, and less disruptive in school. Teenage girls are less likely to get pregnant. In my home county, 47 percent of the babies born in 1998 were illegitimate. We've got to do something about that.

I had an interesting lunch one day with the columnist William Raspberry. I asked him what we could do to help young African-American males. He said one problem is that too many of their mothers don't really believe their children can have a good future. They don't believe it's possible for *their* child. So these young men don't do what they could do, don't try to learn what they could learn. Maybe they fall in with the wrong crowd and get into trouble. They don't have hope. They don't really believe.

Think of all the love and support and all the caring and encouragement you give your own children. Well, some young people have very little of that, and they need to get it from somebody. They need picking up, and they need hope.

Look around your church or wherever you worship and see all the people in the pews. Most have good incomes, they are well-meaning, they want things to be better, they care about children. They believe in God and His command to help children. All we need to do is to match up about 5 percent of these good people with youngsters who need help. To find out how many kids are at risk in your community, ask the schools, the juvenile court counselors, the police department. They know exactly who these young people are. If we care enough and work hard enough, we can find a mentor for every one of them. Let's say it's six hundred youngsters who need help. Well, let's find a mentor for every one of them. Six hundred mentors. We can do that, and we ought to do it. We ought to do nothing less.

If we want our young people to have hope, we must give them help. If we give every one of them help and hope, they can learn. They can have the future they deserve, and North Carolina can be the kind of state we want it to be. We should give them all what my mother gave her students: a belief in themselves and hope for the future.

CHAPTER 9

Our Most Important Enterprise

EDUCATION CAN'T BE just another thing we do. It's the *most important* thing we do. The theme of my 1997 Inaugural, which was held at Broughton High School in Raleigh, was "Education is our future, it's everything."

It's just like with your own children. You know that educating them is the most important thing you do. Their education determines what kind of jobs they are going to have, what kind of people they are going to be, whether they will be good citizens, and whether they will be able to help our society deal with its problems.

People love to talk about their children and grandchildren. You can hear their excitement when they do. You know they'll do anything for their kids; nothing is too good for them. I can talk with the toughest, most hard-nosed businessman in the world, and if I get him talking about his kids, all of a sudden he smiles and it's a whole different world. When we start talking about kids, we establish a relationship and start sharing things that we never shared when we were just doing business.

That's why we can get people involved in the schools. John Gardner, who founded Common Cause and was the nation's first Secretary of Education (the agency was Health, Education, and Welfare then), once described what can happen when we do get involved in the schools:

> It's a public show, with lots and lots of people in the act. That's the way big things get done in this country. When the nation gets excited about something, great energies get released—and not from some central point. They bubble up like geysers from geothermal sources all over the place. All kinds of people and institutions get involved . . . governors, legislators, business and labor leaders, universities, the professions, the media. Then the earth moves.

The earth will move in North Carolina if we get everybody focused on the schools. We'll get the business community working harder to help. We'll get people across the state believing the schools can be better. We'll get parents supporting salary increases for teachers and finding other ways to attract good teachers to their community. We'll be eager to put in the resources that it's going to take to be first in America. We'll insist that teachers be well prepared, value them for their knowledge and skills, and provide time for them to plan and spend the time needed to help all their students. We'll demand that our own community do whatever it takes to fix failing schools and provide students with better teachers, more time to learn, and after-school programs. Whatever it takes.

This striving—this quest—can be the best thing that has happened to us as a people. It can encourage us to care more about each other, to believe more in each other, to help each other. As we focus on our schools, we will be focusing on our children, and it can result in our best side coming out, our best selves.

I'm an optimist about this because I'm an optimist about North Carolina. We believe in children. We believe in basic equality and potential. We believe in doing good, and we believe in helping people. We have this feeling about the "common good" which Bill Friday, the retired President of the University of North Carolina, always said was the secret of the Research Triangle Park. We work at it together because we want to do something for the common good, something for all of our people.

We know we can do it because we have examples of excellence in North Carolina, among them our universities, the Research Triangle Park, and the financial center that Charlotte has become. We know how successful some schools are and the magic that good teachers do.

Part of the reason we haven't done better is that we've been conditioned to failure and poor performance—or average performance. Beginning now, we must change that. We must not accept failing schools or poor schools. We should be upset about it and determined that all of our kids are going to learn. Our kids and everybody else's kids. We must demand change. We must not tolerate a situation where a third to a half of all kids start school not ready to learn, so far behind that they are poor bets to graduate at age eighteen. Not only that, those kids who are so far behind are going to hold *your* kids back. The teacher has to take time away from your children to help the ones who are so poorly prepared. We ought to be furious when our kids are in classrooms so large they can't get individual attention.

Education should also be important to people who don't have children or grandchildren in the schools. They too should pitch in to make our schools the best. For one thing, they may have school-age nieces and nephews. But there also are very practical reasons for them to help. If they care about their job, if they want their company to be competitive worldwide, if they will someday need Social Security and Medicare, then our society has to be productive and our economy has to be strong. If they don't want a lot of their taxes going for jails and prisons and for coping with other social problems, then they too should want all students to learn and be good citizens.

Finally, I think most people want to do the right thing, and many of them would help the schools, even mentor kids, if we appealed to them in the right way. If we could get them to volunteer and mentor, they would take a personal interest in the schools.

This focus on every child is just crucial. We have always had some bright children. A lot of children would do fine if they never even came to school because their parents do so much for them. But our challenge is to get every child to do well—children from troubled homes, children from poor families, children who have been victims of discrimination—every one of them.

If we rise to the challenge, if we refuse to settle for mediocrity, we can make our schools excellent. If we take all five of the goals in this book seriously, if we pursue them all, and if we put in the resources that it's going to take, we can have the best schools in the country.

We will see it happen. We will see our test scores go way up, to the top ten at least. We will see it in teachers' salaries that are in the top ten. We will see it in school violence figures that are negligible. We will see it in teachers who have degrees in their field and are very good at teaching. We will see it in schools that are equally good in rich and poor communities. We will see it in every child learning at grade level or above.

Here is the vision I have for our schools in 2010. They will be places that are attractive and conducive to learning. They will be exciting places where learning is interesting and fun. They will be places where we have very high expectations, where children who have all been given a good start are taught by superb teachers, with the best technology available. They will be places where the community as a whole is constantly focusing on success for all students, with a mentor for every child who needs one and with after-school, weekend, and summer programs for those who need more help or who want to pursue special interests.

Most of all, our schools will be the very *center* of the community, a focus for its citizens, its churches and other congregations, and its businesses. They will be places where excellence is the hallmark—expected not occasionally, but all the time and for every child.

CHAPTER 10

What I've Learned

THIS BOOK IS ABOUT HOPE.

It's about the hope Elsie Brame Hunt gave her students.

It's about the hope thousands of teachers give their students every day in public schools across North Carolina.

It's about the hope I've seen in the eyes of a young man and a young woman when they realize they, too, can learn and be successful and achieve their dreams in life.

It's about the hope we have for our own sons and daughters.

It's about the hope we have for the future of our communities, our state, and our nation.

I know some people are down on the schools and ready to give up on them, maybe because they had a bad experience or their child had a bad teacher. I know some politicians are always looking for a sound bite and an easy answer. I know some people are out to undermine the schools and go to vouchers for private schools.

But I believe the people who give up on public schools are wrong, and I know what I'm talking about.

Few people in public life in America have spent more time than I have studying education, more hours talking to teachers and educators, more days visiting schools, more nights working on new ideas and new approaches, and more afternoons tutoring and mentoring students who need help—and hope.

This book is about what I learned in all those long hours, days, and nights since I started running for Lieutenant Governor of North Carolina nearly thirty years ago.

It's about what I learned listening to teachers, parents, and business people over those years.

It's about what I learned from my teachers, from my children and grandchildren, from my wife, and from my mother.

I've learned that public schools can work.

I've learned that public schools can make our society work.

I've learned that public schools can make our communities and our state better places.

I've learned that every student can learn.

I've learned that there are five goals we must reach—and we must reach them all together:

Goal 1: A Smart Start. Every child must start school healthy and ready to learn.

Goal 2: Excellent Teaching. Every school must have a good principal, and every child must have a good teacher every year.

Goal 3: Safe Schools. Every child must go to a school that is safe and orderly and has caring people working there.

Goal 4: High Student Performance. We must set high, clear, and specific standards for what every student should know and be able to do—and test students to measure their progress.

Goal 5: Community Support. Parents, business people, people of faith, and thousands of mentors and tutors must get involved in the schools, and together we must give all young people the help and the hope they need to succeed in school and in life.

I've learned what it takes, and I've learned that we can do it.

I've learned that North Carolinians can do remarkable things when they set audacious goals and work together to achieve them.

Above all, I've learned that North Carolina *can* have the best schools in America.

As we enter a new century, I challenge you and I challenge all North Carolinians to believe that we can be first in

America in education by 2010, to make it our common goal, and to dedicate ourselves to making it happen—for our children, for our grandchildren, and for all the generations of North Carolinians to come.

Acknowledgments

So many people have contributed so much to this book, it would be impossible to recognize them all. Each page reflects the passion of North Carolina teachers, business executives, parents, students, and citizens, as well as the best thinking of many national leaders.

I want to personally thank all those who have taken the time to help us chart the path to making North Carolina's schools first in America. I am grateful to:

• North Carolina's teachers and principals, who hold our children's future in their hands.

• Decision-makers who are building the foundation for our success: members of the General Assembly, the Education Cabinet, the State Board of Education, the University of North Carolina Board of Governors, the State Board of Community Colleges, Independent Colleges and Universities, the North Carolina Partnership for Children, and other public bodies.

• Business leaders, including those who serve on the North Carolina Business Council of Management and Development, North Carolina Citizens for Business and Industry, and the North Carolina Business Committee for Education; those involved in local business-school partnerships, chambers of commerce, and Smart Start partnerships; those who adopt schools or otherwise contribute to education through their businesses; and those who encourage their employees to do the same.

• The thousands of parents and citizens who volunteer in the schools, whether it's to mentor a student, chaperone a field trip, or serve in government—particularly those who sit on local school boards and county commissions.

I have been especially blessed by the men and women on my staff during my sixteen years as Governor; much of our success in improving North Carolina's schools is due to their work. I particularly thank Wayne McDevitt, Lynda McCulloch, Cecil Banks, Karen Garr, Warren Miller, Jenni Owen, Dana Pope, Anthony Petty, Adam Shapiro, Rachel Perry, and Sean Walsh for all their hard work on this book. I also owe special thanks to Karen Ponder and Debbie Lee Averitt.

As he has in projects throughout the years, Gary Pearce has gone the extra mile in getting this book ready to print.

To all of you, I offer heartfelt thanks.

J.H.

About the Author

James B. Hunt Jr. served sixteen years as Governor of North Carolina (1977–1985, 1993–2001). He is a nationally recognized leader in education and has led his state through twenty years of dramatic economic change. Serving a historic fourth term as Governor, he has been at the forefront of education reform in his state and in the nation.

He has particularly focused on early childhood development and improving the quality of teaching in America. His Smart Start initiative, a nonprofit, public-private partnership rooted in each of the state's one hundred counties, provides quality child care, health care, and family support for each child who needs it. It is funded primarily by the state but is also supported heavily by private corporations and individuals. Smart Start has been visited and studied by early childhood leaders from all fifty states and many foreign countries. It has received the prestigious Innovations in America Government Award from the Ford Foundation and the John F. Kennedy School of Government at Harvard University.

Governor Hunt has devoted much of his life to excellence in teaching in the United States. In 1985 he co-chaired with David Hamburg the "Committee of 50," which led to the Carnegie Forum on Education and the Economy and eventually to the National Board for Professional Teaching Standards. He served as chairman of that board for ten years, developing standards for what accomplished teachers in America need to know and be able to do and assessments to "board-certify" them. Governor Hunt also serves as the chairman of the National Commission on Teaching and America's Future. Its report in 1996, *What Matters Most: Teaching for America's Future,* is stimulating major changes in teacher education programs and public policies that advance teaching.

A strong supporter of high standards in public schools, Governor Hunt has served as chairman of the National Education Goals Panel and vice chairman of the board of Achieve Inc. He has put into place in North Carolina one of the nation's most rigorous approaches to measuring student performance, requiring mastery for promotion and graduation and providing assistance to turn around failing schools.

His state's economic gains from educational improvement have been impressive. North Carolina has regularly led the nation in new job creation per capita and in foreign investment. He has focused on new technologies by establishing the North Carolina School of Science and Mathematics, the Microelectronics Center of North Carolina, and the North Carolina Biotechnology Center. In higher education, he serves as chairman of the National Center for Public Policy and Higher Education located in San Jose, California. He is also a Trustee of the Carnegie Corporation of New York.

Governor Hunt holds B.A. and M.S. degrees from North Carolina State University and a J.D. degree from the University of North Carolina at Chapel Hill.

In 1964–66, he and his family lived in Katmandu, Nepal, where he served as a Ford Foundation Economic Advisor to His Majesty's Government. He has served on the Commission on US-Japan Relations for the 21st century, and, working with the Asia Society, co-chairs the National Commission on Asia in the Schools.

Governor Hunt and his wife, Carolyn, live on their beef cattle farm in eastern North Carolina. They have four children and eight grandchildren.

© 2001 Governor James B. Hunt Jr.
All rights reserved.

The paper used in this publication meets the minimum requirements of American National Standards for Information Science—Permanence of Paper for Printed materials, ANSI Z39.48—1984. ∞

This book has been designed by Kachergis Book Design, Pittsboro, North Carolina.

Cover photograph © 2000 Bob Rives

Cataloging-in-Publication Data
Hunt, James B., 1937–
    First in America : an education governor challenges North Carolina / by Governor James B. Hunt, Jr. — Raleigh, NC : First in American Foundation, [2001]
    Library of Congress Card Number: 00-111657
      p. ; cm.
    "January 2001."
    1. Education—Aims and objectives—North Carolina.   2. Early childhood education—North Carolina.   3. Smart Start Program (N.C.)   4. Education and state—North Carolina.   5. Educational change—North Carolina—Philosophy.   6. Public schools—North Carolina.   I. North Carolina Governor (1977–1985; 1993–2001 : Hunt)   II. First in America Foundation.
LC90.N8 H86 2001
370.9756—dc21

00-111657

For more information on the first-in-America challenge, or to obtain copies of this book, please call 866-850-2010, or visit the First in America Foundation website at *www.firstinamericafoundation.com*.